Copyright © 2020 by Jazmine Vega
All rights reserved.
Printed in the United States of America.
No reproduction of this book in part or whole, scanned, or distributed in any printed or electronic form
without consent from Jazmine Vega.
Disclaimer: All persons fictitious.
978-1-63760-5455

Thank you for your love, support, and contribution.

Marvin Zanders Jr.

Tanisha McVay

Zhanne' Easter

Sasha Robinson

Lacey Vega

Dale McVay

This book is dedicated to
Ariana
Tavaris
Sincere
Micah
Dalena
Zariyah
Prielle
Prejour
Amaiya
Nyla
Sekani

Today was a big day for Barbara Jean. It was her first day of Kindergarten. Barbara Jean was excited for school because it meant she was a big girl. She couldn't wait to meet her teacher and make new friends.

"Barbara Jean, I am going to drop you off at school and your daddy will pick you up today. I want you to have fun and be a good girl," said Mom.

Barbara Jean started to feel anxious as she watched her mom finish making her lunch. "I will be a good girl today mommy," Barbara Jean said softly.

Barbara Jean walked to the classroom with a huge smile on her face. "Bye Mommy, see you later!"

"Hi! I'm Ms. Clarke. What's your name?" "Hi! My name is Barbara Jean, but you can call me BJ." "Hi BJ! Why don't you walk over to the yellow table and find your name tag," said Ms. Clarke.

Barbara Jean found her name and put it on her shirt. At that moment she knew she was officially a big girl. "You found your name! Great Job!" Ms. Clarke said with excitement.

Barbara Jean went to take a seat on the alphabet rug and couldn't believe her eyes. Brandon was sitting on the letter "B"! Ms. Clarke! Ms. Clarke! Barbara Jean yelled in disbelief. "

He's sitting on my letter. "Get off my letter!" screamed Barbara Jean. "I was here first. You're mean Barbara Jean." Said Brandon.

Barbara Jean, one of our classroom rules is "use your library voice," explained Ms. Clarke. "Please do not yell in class or at our friends."
"I'm sorry, but he's on MY letter."

"Do you want to sit together?" asked Brandon, as he sat there concerned if Barbara Jean would start to cry. "Yes, please," Barbara Jean said with a smile. "That was nice of you Brandon. Thank you for being a great friend," said Ms. Clarke.

Everyone had so much fun singing songs and reading books but now it was snack time. " Okay friends, have a seat and let's all eat snack," said Ms.Clarke.

Barbara Jean sat in the purple chair. That is her favorite color.

Barbara Jean was happy to have apples as a snack. She accidentally dropped her apples on the carpet. She was really sad until she saw Summer had apples too.

Barbara Jean reached over and took an apple slice off Summer's plate. "Hey! That's my apple! You're mean Barbara Jean!" yelled Summer. "But I don't have any more apples," said Barbara Jean.

"Ms. Clarke, Barbara Jean took my apple," Summer said sadly. "Barbara Jean, did you take Summer's apple?" Ms. Clarke asked.

"I dropped mine and I wanted another one." "Okay friends, let's all remember one of the classroom rules is "do not take things from our friends," said Ms. Clarke.

Barbara Jean next time you can ask Summer to share," explained Ms. Clarke.
"Okay Ms. Clarke," said Barbara Jean.

"Summer, I am sorry for taking your apple," said Barbara Jean.
"Thank you for saying sorry. Next time we can share," said Summer.

Snack time was over and the children were ready to play outside. Barbara Jean remembered seeing swings when her mom drove her to school. She couldn't wait to play on the swing.

Barbara Jean ran to the swing but Ava got there first. "No, Ava No! I wanted that swing!" Barbara Jean pushed Ava. "You're mean Barbara Jean!" cried Ava.

"Why are you crying Ava?" asked Ms.Clarke. "Barbara Jean pushed me off the swing!" Ava said sadly. "Did you push Ava?" Ms. Clarke asked.

"Yes, I did. She was on my swing," said Barbara Jean. Ms. Clarke reminded Barbara Jean of the classroom rule, "do not hit your friends", and asked Barbara Jean to say sorry to Ava.

"Well, Ava is not my friend because she took my swing!" Barbara Jean said with anger.

Ms. Clarke explained to Barbara Jean that the swing was for everyone to share.

"I am sorry for pushing you Ava. Can we be friends? " said Barbara Jean. "Okay. Come on, let's go take turns swinging," Ava said.

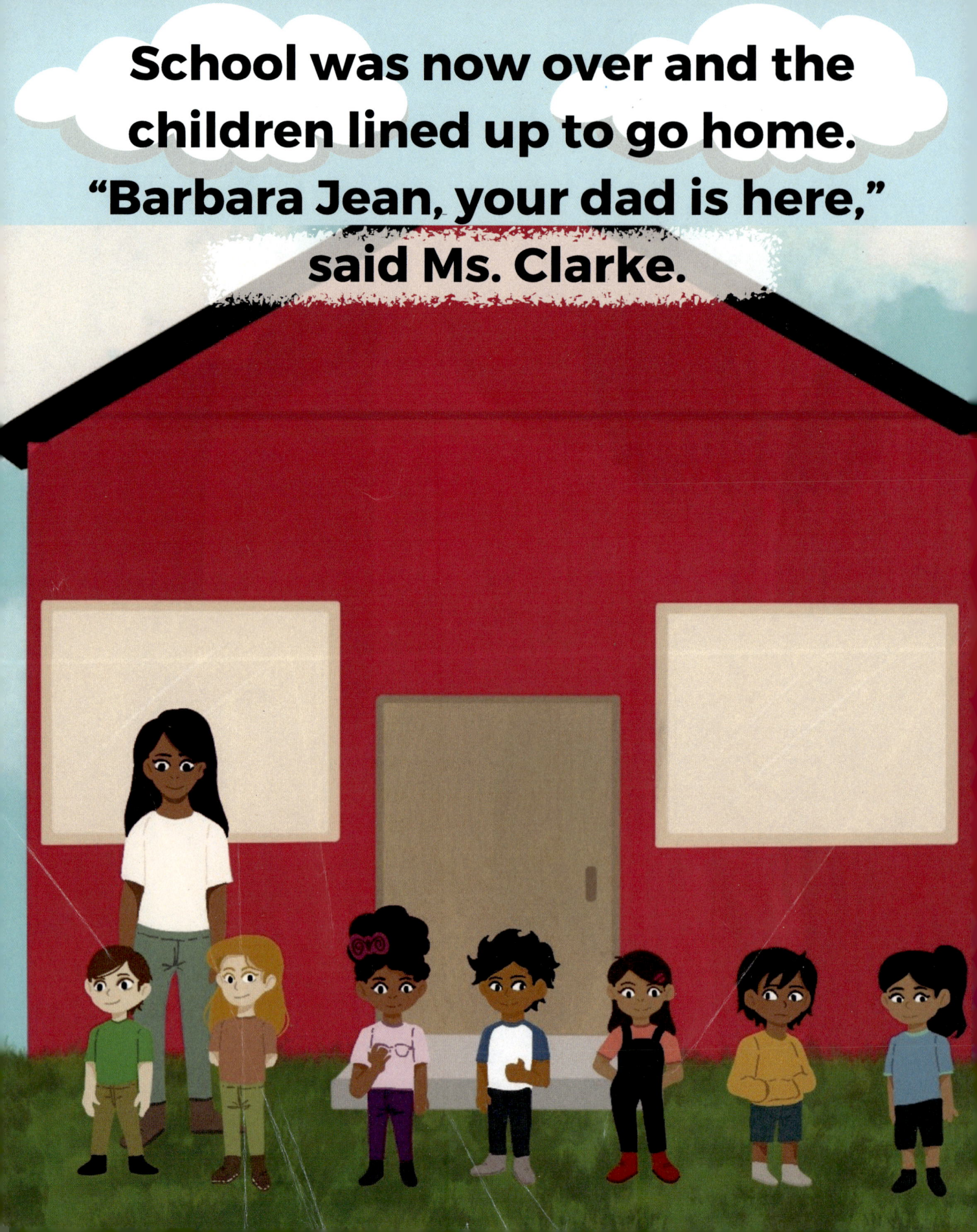

"Daddy! Barbara Jean ran to her daddy and gave him a big hug. "Hi BJ! Did you have fun today?" asked Daddy. "Yes I did." I sat on the letter B for Barbara Jean. I ate apples, and played on the swings! I can't wait to come back tomorrow!

Made in the USA
Monee, IL
30 January 2021